Away in a Manger

The Christmas Story from a Nativity Scene Lamb's Point of View

David B. Biebel

AWAY IN A MANGER
The Christmas Story From a Nativity Scene Lamb's Point of View
LARGE PRINT EDITION
Copyright © 2017 by David B. Biebel

Published by:
Healthy Life Press • Denver, CO 80219
www.healthylifepress.com

Illustrations and cover by Marina Calin
All artwork © 2017 Marina Calin & Healthy Life Press

Interior Design: Judy Johnson

Printed in the United States of America

No part of this publication may be reproduced, stored in a retrieval system, or transmitted in any form or by any means without the prior written consent of the publisher.

Library of Congress Cataloging-in-Publication Data
Biebel, David B.
Away in a Manger: The Christmas Story from a Nativity Scene Lamb's Point of View

ISBN 978-1-939267-85-6

1. RELIGION / Holidays / Christmas & Advent
2. RELIGION / Holidays / Christian

We have chosen to use the New Living Translation (NLT) in this book because we expect that it will be read by adults to young children, and since they are the primary audience we believe the NLT will be easier for them to understand. All Scriptures quoted in this book are from The Holy Bible, New Living Translation copyright © 1996, 2004, 2007, 2013 by Tyndale House Foundation. Used by permission of Tyndale House Publishers Inc., Carol Stream, Illinois 60188. All rights reserved.

This full-color book is available in two sizes, 6.5x6.5 and 8x10 (Large Print) The ISBN for the 8x10 (Large Print) version is: 978-1-939267-85-6, $15.99. The ISBN for the 6.5x6.5 version is: 978-1939267399, $12.99.

For All My Children, and Yours as Well

Author's Introduction

This book had at least three years' gestation, as I tried to imagine a new way to tell the Christmas story while at the same time remaining true to the Scriptural accounts related to Jesus' birth. Strangely enough, once the writing began, the storyline developed without much intrusion by its "author," and what emerged was far beyond what he had envisioned. In fact, even after the first edition had been released, the storyline continued to develop itself, suggesting that a sequel may be needed in order to follow the adventures of a lamb named Ransom and all his newfound friends.

     This book reads like a family-oriented novella that parents can enjoy, themselves, or read to their children. Its context is a live Christmas Nativity scene as experienced by a very inquisitive lamb who has been chosen to participate.

     Many Old Testament and New Testament references to Jesus' birth are included, the net result being an educational experience for children and adults. For all, it gives a fresh view of the true meaning of Christmas.

     A salvation invitation is included, as well, with a prayer to receive Christ, for as John said: "But as many as received him, to them gave he power to become the sons of God, even to them that believe on his name." (KJV)

     Please let me make it clear that nothing in this partly fictional account is meant to imply that animals can inherit eternal life. In this novel, they are facilitators of faith for all the humans who come to see the Nativity Scene, because just seeing them and the stable and the manger and the baby and his parents takes the message of Christ's birth past the mind and directly to the heart. Enjoy, and be blessed!

Contents

Chapter 1: Ransom is Chosen — 1

Chapter 2: The Pastor Takes a Camel Ride — 9

Chapter 3: Ransom Meets Jenny — 19

Chapter 4: Angelic Visitations — 27

Chapter 5: A Child is Born — 43

Chapter 1

Ransom is Chosen

Once upon a time, on the edge of a beautiful mountain meadow in Colorado, a baby lamb was born. His Mommy named him "Ransom."

This happened in the spring, when everything was green, except there were so many shades of green that the sheep who lived there didn't really have enough names for all the greens.

There was the unique green of new aspen leaves, and the light to dark varieties of the delicious grasses and clover. The evergreens were nice, of course, for shade and protection during storms, but not so good for munching upon.

To most of the sheep, green was just green, but not to Ransom. For Ransom was a questioner, and one question just seemed to naturally lead to another question. And of course his Mommy answered every question that she could, shaking her head from time to time, as sheep often do when they are amazed.

While most of the other lambs ate whatever happened to come in front of their mouth as they ambled along, Ransom's Mommy was very careful to teach him which of the plants could make him sick, and which were delicious and healthy.

Her favorite was clover, and that's what she and Ransom ate most of the time in addition to the basic meadow grasses that were so lush and yummy in the spring.

Ransom noticed so many things that the other lambs never seemed to notice; especially the wildflowers that transformed the meadow into a beautiful medley of color, which seemed to change almost daily as if he were looking through a kaleidoscope. He liked the Indian Paintbrush for some reason, and the Blue Flax, Queen's Crown, Bistort, and Elephant's Head, but his favorites were the Columbines, so exquisitely colored and so delicate. He loved to sniff them, but of course he never ate any. Some things are so beautiful they simply shouldn't be eaten.

The meadow's "clothing" changed slowly as spring turned into summer, and the grasses started to dry out from the hot midday sun. As this happened, Ransom was thankful for the snow-fed stream that bordered the meadow. There he could get a nice cool drink any time he needed one.

But when he stepped into the darker shadows of the evergreens and brush along the stream, he always stayed alert for predators like the bear that had taken away one of his friends in the spring, and the coyotes that seemed to be all around them in the night time, yapping and carrying on. He had heard that mountain lions sometimes prowled the area along the stream, also, looking to lunch upon a lamb or full-grown sheep that had wandered just a little bit further from the flock than was safe.

With all these dangerous predators lurking about, Ransom was thankful that the shepherd was always there, and for the shepherd's guard dogs, three Great Pyrenees that stayed on the perimeter of the herd day and night and were big enough and aggressive enough to chase just about anything away.

One day in late summer the shepherd rounded up all the sheep, including all the lambs, and took them down a trail that led to the ranch that he worked for. "Mommy," Ransom asked, "where are we going?"

"Well," Mommy said, "the rancher who is our real master is going to send most of the lambs and some of the rams to market."

"Are they going shopping?"

"No, my son. They are going to fulfill their destiny."

"Are we going, too?"

"I don't know for sure, because it is up to the rancher. But there is a chance that he will choose us to appear in the live Christmas Nativity program that his church sponsors every year. That's why I named you 'Ransom,' and I know that he is looking forward to meeting you."

Later that afternoon, after the five-mile descent of the mountain trail, the sheep, shepherd, and dogs all arrived at the ranch. Ransom and his Mommy lingered near the back of the group, as the sheep and lambs were separated, with the lambs being loaded into several large trucks that were waiting. Some of the adult sheep also went along, in another truck.

After what seemed like a long time, the rancher, whose name was Hank, finally came over to Ransom and his Mommy. Hank seemed like a nice person as he felt gently through Ransom's curly fleece all the way to his skin.

He checked Ransom's legs also, and his head, and then

he stepped back just a little and said, "This lamb will be perfect for the Christmas Nativity display! Once again, Maria," he said to Mommy, "you have produced a lamb without defect, spot, or blemish. You are special among the ewes."

Then he put his hands on both their heads, closed his eyes, and prayed, "Father in heaven, I pray that these sheep from our flock will bring glory to you, when we celebrate the birth of your Son in just a few months. Amen."

Chapter 2

The Pastor Takes a Camel Ride

In two shakes of a lamb's tail, it was time to construct the stable that would be the focal point of the live nativity scene. From time to time, the rancher took the animals along to get them used to the surroundings, since he knew that during the week leading up to Christmas Eve the crowd could become somewhat rowdy. It was a good kind of rowdy, as in clapping and sometimes cheering and always singing along with the Christmas carols that played in the background when no narration was taking place.

A cow, a donkey, Ransom and his Mommy, and even a camel got to visit the construction site, traveling comfortably in the back of the rancher's trailer.

The nativity scene was being built on a small hill that sloped down and away from the front of the church building to the street. From time to time Pastor Peter would wander on over with some hot chocolate and cookies for the volunteers, who thankfully ate and drank since the weather had been turning gradually colder as they worked.

The pastor seemed to really enjoy patting and rubbing all the animals. But when the rancher invited him to mount the camel for a ride around the parking lot, at first the pastor declined; then, on second thought, he climbed aboard with a boost from Hank, and everybody got a good laugh as he held on more tightly than might have been necessary until he, the camel, and the rancher returned. The camel's reward was an apple and a carrot.

"Whew!" exclaimed the pastor. "Those wise men who came from the East must have been pretty sore when they finally got there! Ouch! I would have to have a padded saddle to ride half a mile compared to the hundreds of miles they came in search of The King of the Jews."

He then knelt down to run his fingers through Ransom's fleece. "How soft," he said, stroking the lamb's head. With his hand gently caressing Ransom's nose, he turned to the rancher. "Perfect again, Hank. He and his mommy

will add so much authenticity to the scene. The children always love to pat the lamb. And it makes everything else so real to them. Does he have a name?"

Hank winked at Maria, and said, "Ransom is his name."

"Absolutely, right on!" exclaimed the pastor."

"Mommy," Ransom whispered. "How does he know my name?"

"I told him," she whispered back.

"He understands us?"

"Of course," she replied. "Don't you understand him? Some humans, but not all of them, understand us; and we understand them. Now shush."

The pastor came around and knelt right in front of Ransom, looking him directly in the eyes. Ordinarily, Ransom would only let Mommy or the shepherd do that, but there was something about this man; something a lot like what he thought only Mommy and the Shepherd could communicate without saying a word. Love, that was it. But why this man should care for him, he didn't know.

Ransom's question came out of his mouth before he could stop himself, "Why do you love me?" he asked, his question sounding like, "Baa, baa, baa?" to most of the volunteers.

"Because," the pastor whispered, so only Ransom and

Maria could hear, "you will help me retell the greatest story ever told. I say a lot of words to the people about Jesus through the year, but there's nothing quite as effective in getting past their minds to their hearts as a live rendition of the nativity."

Then, without hardly pausing and with his hand still on Ransom's head, the pastor started to pray in a much louder voice, "Lord," he said, "we dedicate ourselves and all this work and all these participants, from volunteers to these animals here, to serve you well over these next few days, and especially to remind all who visit this display about the true meaning of Christmas, both to us and to you. Amen."

Soon after all the animals had snacked on some hay, giving the volunteers an opportunity to pat them and scratch their backs, Rancher Hank herded them onto the trailer for their ride back to the ranch.

Along the way, Ransom had many questions for his Mommy: "Mommy, who is Jesus?" he asked. "The pastor said that I would be helping him tell people about Jesus, but I don't know who Jesus is."

"Jesus is the central figure in the nativity scene," she replied. "In fact, it's really all about him; the rest of us are like the frame of a beautiful piece of art.

"The word 'nativity' means the occasion of a person's birth. Did you notice the manger toward the back of the stable? Ordinarily, a manger is where the cattle come to eat. In our case, a baby who represents Jesus will be laid in that manger, so people can see the way it happened about 2000 years ago."

"Didn't the pastor call him 'The King of the Jews?'"

"Yes, dear, and that he was," Maria answered.

"Well, if you ask me, that seems like a pretty slobbery place for a newborn baby," Ransom said.

His mother laughed in spite of herself. "Yes, it might have been slobbery, but at least it was soft, and the stable was probably warm from the heat of the animals inside. Besides, it was the best they could do, because they were quite poor."

"Mary, his mother, and Joseph, his earthly 'father,' had to travel to Bethlehem because a census was being taken and that was Joseph's home town. They traveled from Nazareth, where they lived, using a safe route that may have been as long as 90 miles.

"Mary, who was about to deliver her first child, would have found it very hard to walk all that way, so it is thought that she rode at least part of that way on a donkey.

"That's why sometimes there's a donkey in the nativity scene. And when they got to Bethlehem, there was no room for them in the inn, so after she gave birth to Jesus, she placed him in a manger."

"So we'll be helping the pastor tell people about a baby named Jesus?"

"Yes," Mommy said, "but this baby grew into a man whose life and death and resurrection changed the history of the world. 'Resurrection' means that after he was dead, he came back to life again, proving that he really is the Son of God.'"

"You mean he is the Son of the same God who made the mountains and the meadow and the flowers, and even me, like you've told me many times?"

"Yes, Ransom dear," the lamb's Mommy replied. "The same God. The only God."

"But you never told me he has a Son."

"I thought that being in this nativity program would be a good way for you to learn."

"Wow," said Ransom, "I can't wait to hear the rest of the story!"

Chapter 3

Ransom Meets Jenny

The rest of the story began three nights later, when just after dark, the pastor took his spot to the right of the stable as you looked at it, next to the stack of hay.

"Hello friends," he said, using the built-in but very cleverly disguised public address system. "Welcome to the fourth annual live nativity program, presented by Christ's Community Church, of which I am the pastor. Tonight's introductory presentation will focus on the background of the nativity scene idea, and also the background of the birth of Jesus, which we find in the Old Testament prophets.

"In terms of the nativity display itself, it was first created in 1223 A.D. by Francis of Assisi, an Italian Roman Catholic Friar who wanted to promote the true meaning of

Christmas. The idea caught on very quickly, and today thousands of displays like ours can be found worldwide, sponsored by many denominations of the Christian church. Some involve live characters, but many others involve figurines representing most of the characters you see here tonight: Jesus in the manger; Mary, his mother, and Joseph, his earthly father; shepherds and their sheep; angels; and quite often three wise men and one or more camels."

"You can find the names of this year's participants in the program you've received. The Scriptures are also included, to make it easier to follow along with me in a few moments when we get to them."

He paused so the ushers could give programs to those who needed them. Then he continued, "With that little bit of background, let's dedicate this presentation to the Lord, whose birth we are celebrating in this special way.

"Lord," he prayed, "we dedicate this entire event to you, now. Through the special focus that this display provides, may we set aside other, more self-oriented thoughts about Christmas and all the hopes and plans we may have, and for just these few minutes each night, keep our minds stayed upon you! Amen."

Now there's an interesting phrase, Ransom thought. *I wonder what it means to have your mind "stayed" on someone. When we were in the mountains and Mommy told me to stay, I knew that either she wanted me to remain close to her in order to stay safe from danger, or that I should stay by her side so I wouldn't wander off and get lost. I'll have to ask her later.*

"You know," the pastor said, "it was the prophet Isaiah who said the Lord would keep us in perfect peace, if our mind was stayed on him. I am reading tonight from the New Living Translation, and we'll start our review of the Old Testament statements about Jesus with Isaiah, who wrote:

> *. . . the Lord himself will give you the sign. Look! The virgin will conceive a child! She will give birth to a son and will call him Immanuel (which means "God is with us").*

"Now, this would take a miracle, would you not agree? We all know that's not the way it works; but God is in the miracle business and that is how he decided to make it work. Then, just a few verses later, the prophet added this":

For a child is born to us,
   a son is given to us.
The government will rest on his shoulders.
   And he will be called:
Wonderful Counselor, Mighty God,
   Everlasting Father, Prince of Peace.

"What a marvelous description of the Lord Jesus Christ, given approximately 700 years before he was born! But Isaiah was not the only prophet who spoke of Jesus," he continued. "Jeremiah wrote":

"For the time is coming,"
   says the Lord,
"when I will raise up a righteous descendant
   from King David's line.

He will be a King who rules with wisdom.
   He will do what is just and right
     throughout the land."

"And the prophet Micah even predicted where the Messiah, Jesus, would be born":

But you, O Bethlehem Ephrathah,
   are only a small village among all the
      people of Judah.
Yet a ruler of Israel,
   whose origins are in the distant past,
   will come from you on my behalf.

"There are more than 40 prophecies about Jesus in the Old Testament, but most of them have to do with his ministry and the meaning of his life as the Lamb of God who takes away the sins of the world, in the words of John the Baptist, which he accomplished by giving his life, a ransom for all who would believe in him. We'll say more about that tomorrow night."

Ransom had almost fainted at the pastor's last words, but he managed to maintain his composure as the crowd of adults launched into singing Christmas carols and a gaggle of children crowded around him, caressing his soft fleece and loving him in their own special way.

This felt so wonderful that he almost missed the words of a young girl, who whispered in his ear, "Ransom, you are such a beautiful lamb. I wish I could take you home so we could run and laugh and play in the meadow behind my home."

"How do you know my name?" Ransom replied.

"I just do, like I can understand you and you can understand me. My name is. . . ."

"Jenny," said Ransom. "Somehow I knew."

"Amazing," she said. "But there are so many other kids who want to pat you. I'll hope to see you tomorrow night . . . if my mother will let me come."

"Why wouldn't she?" he asked.

"Well, we're not very religious," Jenny replied. "I think maybe long ago some church people judged her for having me, when she wasn't married. I better go now," she whispered.

A few minutes later, Hank rounded up the animals and led them to the trailer. As soon as they were on the road, Ransom turned to his Mommy and asked, "What did the pastor mean when he said 'the Lamb of God who takes away the sins of the world,' and 'who gave his life a ransom for many?'"

"Well," she replied, "it's all part of the story of Jesus, the baby in the manger who grew up to be the Savior of all who believe in him. Many years before his birth, the Jewish people escaped their bondage in Egypt when they followed instructions from God through Moses to sacrifice a year-old lamb (or a goat) without blemish on a certain day and to place its blood on the doorposts of their homes. When the angel of the Lord came to strike the first-born of the Egyptians, he would 'pass over' the homes with the blood.

"The passover lamb gave its life in order for the people of Israel to be ransomed from their captivity. Jesus gave his life to ransom humanity from its captivity to sin. I knew this when I named you Ransom."

"Does that mean I'm going to be sacrificed," Ransom asked.

"No, dear," his Mommy replied. "No more sacrifices are needed, because Jesus' death was the ultimate sacrifice for the sins of all who believe in him.

"You and I and the others in the nativity program are just symbols, in a sense, to remind the people of the true meaning of what happened when God took on human flesh in the person of a baby named Jesus, who, when he had become a man, showed mankind what God is really like, and what it means to follow his way."

Chapter 4

Angelic Visitations

The second night of the nativity program more people were in attendance, both adults and children. The pastor took his place and then continued from where he had left off the previous night.

"Last evening," he began, "we discussed the history of the nativity scene, and also read a few of the 40 or so Old Testament prophecies that described the Coming One, often called the Messiah. The prophets predicted that he would be born of a virgin, in Bethlehem, and that he would be of the tribe of Judah, a descendant of the Old Testament King, David. This is why Matthew is so careful to start his gospel by tracing the lineage of Jesus. You can read along with me in your programs, and bear with me—genealogies are not my favorite reading material, except in this one case. But before we begin tonight's reading, let's dedicate this time to the Lord."

He prayed, "Lord, help us understand more clearly, as a result of tonight's program, that the One who took on human flesh and was born in Bethlehem, which means 'house of bread,' the bread of life who satisfies our deepest hunger, which is to know you and to be known by you. Amen."

He paused, opened his Bible to Matthew 1, commenting, "This genealogy is thought by many to be a very boring passage, so I won't read the whole thing, only parts of it that I want to emphasize, and you can follow along in your program. And, as a reminder, I will be continuing to read tonight from the New Living Translation:

> *This is a record of the ancestors of Jesus the Messiah, a descendant of David and of Abraham:*
>
> *Abraham was the father of Isaac.*
> *Isaac was the father of Jacob.*
> *Jacob was the father of Judah*
>   *and his brothers.*

Judah was the father of Perez and Zerah
  (whose mother was Tamar).
Perez was the father of Hezron.
Hezron was the father of Ram.
Ram was the father of Amminadab.
Amminadab was the father of Nahshon.
Nahshon was the father of Salmon.
Salmon was the father of Boaz
  (whose mother was Rahab).
Boaz was the father of Obed
  (whose mother was Ruth).
Obed was the father of Jesse.
Jesse was the father of King David.
David was the father of Solomon
  (whose mother was Bathsheba,
  the widow of Uriah). . . .

(Now, skip with me to verse 16):

Jacob was the father of Joseph,
  the husband of Mary.
Mary gave birth to Jesus,
  who is called the Messiah.

> *All those listed above include fourteen generations from Abraham to David, fourteen from David to the Babylonian exile, and fourteen from the Babylonian exile to the Messiah.*

"This part of Matthew is extremely important because it establishes that Jesus had the credentials necessary to be the Messiah: son of Abraham; son of David. If this were not true, he could not have been the Messiah. You would expect the Messiah to come from an impeccable family tree, wouldn't you? But the first six verses name a liar, a conniver, a woman who seduced her father-in-law (thus causing him to commit incest), a prostitute, a Gentile, two adulterers (one of whom was a murderer, also). I won't recount all the gory details in this context, since there are so many children present. While it's true that Matthew was establishing the lineage of Jesus, God used this 'boring' section to say something really awesome: *He can use anyone to accomplish his purposes, and 'anyone' includes you and me, with all our shortcomings and failures.*

"But now, let's continue with the part from Matthew 1 that relates specifically to our nativity scene":

This is how Jesus the Messiah was born. His mother, Mary, was engaged to be married to Joseph. But before the marriage took place, while she was still a virgin, she became pregnant through the power of the Holy Spirit. Joseph, to whom she was engaged, was a righteous man and did not want to disgrace her publicly, so he decided to break the engagement quietly.

As he considered this, an angel of the Lord appeared to him in a dream. "Joseph, son of David," the angel said, "do not be afraid to take Mary as your wife. For the child within her was conceived by the Holy Spirit. And she will have a son, and you are to name him Jesus, for he will save his people from their sins."

All of this occurred to fulfill the Lord's message through his prophet:

"Look! The virgin will conceive a child!

*She will give birth to a son,
and they will call him Immanuel,
which means 'God is with us.'"*

When Joseph woke up, he did as the angel of the Lord commanded and took Mary as his wife. But he did not have . . . relations with her until her son was born. And Joseph named him Jesus.

"To me, one amazing part of this passage is the message of the angel in Joseph's dream," the pastor said. "Joseph knew that Mary, to whom he was engaged, was pregnant, and that he was not the father. But he was a just man and he loved Mary, so he was going to divorce her secretly.

"Have you ever wondered how the angel knew what Joseph was thinking? The point is that God knows us through and through—our thoughts before we have them; our words before we say them; our deeds before we do them. That is definitely a sobering truth, and one that should motivate us to keep our mind stayed on him, as I said last night, for when we do that, we are so much more likely to live a life that honors him.

"But of course there's another side to this story, and that is presented by Dr. Luke, who must have interviewed Mary in order to obtain the details that are included. Reading from Luke 1, in the New Living Translation:

> *In the sixth month of Elizabeth's pregnancy, God sent the angel Gabriel to Nazareth, a village in Galilee, to a virgin named Mary. She was engaged to be married to a man named Joseph, a descendant of King David. Gabriel appeared to her and said, "Greetings, favored woman! The Lord is with you!"*

> *Confused and disturbed, Mary tried to think what the angel could mean. "Don't be afraid, Mary," the angel told her, "for you have found favor with God! You will conceive and give birth to a son, and you will name him Jesus. He will be very great and will be called the Son of the Most High. The Lord God will give him the throne of his ancestor David. And he will reign over Israel forever; his Kingdom will never end!"*

Mary asked the angel, "But how can this happen? I am a virgin."

The angel replied, "The Holy Spirit will come upon you, and the power of the Most High will overshadow you. So the baby to be born will be holy, and he will be called the Son of God. What's more, your relative Elizabeth has become pregnant in her old age! People used to say she was barren, but she has conceived a son and is now in her sixth month. For the word of God will never fail."

Mary responded, "I am the Lord's servant. May everything you have said about me come true." And then the angel left her.

"So Mary went to visit Elizabeth and this is what happened next," the pastor said:

She entered the house and greeted Elizabeth. At the sound of Mary's greeting, Elizabeth's child leaped within her, and Elizabeth was filled with the Holy Spirit.

Elizabeth gave a glad cry and exclaimed to Mary, "God has blessed you above all women, and your child is blessed. Why am I so honored, that the mother of my Lord should visit me? When I heard your greeting, the baby in my womb jumped for joy. You are blessed because you believed that the Lord would do what he said."

Mary responded,
"Oh, how my soul praises the Lord.
  How my spirit rejoices in God my Savior!
For he took notice of his lowly servant girl,
  and from now on all generations
  will call me blessed.
For the Mighty One is holy,
  and he has done great things for me.
He shows mercy from generation to
  generation to all who fear him.
His mighty arm has done tremendous things!

He has scattered the proud
and haughty ones.
He has brought down princes
from their thrones
and exalted the humble.
He has filled the hungry with good things
and sent the rich away
with empty hands.
He has helped his servant Israel
and remembered to be merciful.
For he made this promise to our ancestors,
to Abraham and his children forever."

As if on signal, someone started playing a guitar and singing "Away in a Manger," while the adults and teens joined in loudly, and the children ran forward to pet the animals. Many of them headed right for Ransom, who was watching intently for Jenny, but she was nowhere to be seen. His countenance fell, well it fell as much as any lamb's countenance can fall, but he knew he had to pay attention to the others, whose attention took away his sadness in a very short time.

On the way back to the ranch, Ransom asked, "Mommy, what is 'lineage'? Do I have one of those?"

"Everyone does, dear," she replied. "It means your parentage or family tree. This helps place a person like Jesus in history, and shows how his lineage could be traced back to King David, which was one element of the prophecies about him."

"Is a family tree like a spruce or an oak?" he asked.

"Well now, I've never thought about it that way. An oak loses its leaves each year, but it also grows a little bit with each new spring, and it branches out so if you look up from the trunk, you can see branches in all directions, some of them with their own branches off the main branch. Since the phrase 'family tree' is using the idea of a tree that branches out, I'd say it's more like an oak than a spruce."

"So where am I on our family tree?"

"You're like a bud at the very end of one of the branches. And if you become a father someday, you'll then become part of a branch that has grown even longer."

"And you are part of the same branch, only a little closer to the main trunk. I think I understand. . . ." Ransom stopped mid-sentence. "But I must also have a father. You've never mentioned him."

"His name was Virgil, and for many years he was the master ram of our herd. But this spring, just after you were born, and I was not strong enough to defend you, he gave his life to save us from a mountain lion. He won the battle, but the lion wounded him so badly that there was nothing that could be done to save him."

"Oh," Ransom replied, not knowing if he should be sad he'd never gotten to know his father, or proud that his father had laid down his life to save the herd.

And for the first time in a long time, he couldn't think of anything else to say.

CHAPTER 5

A Child is Born

On the final night of the live nativity display, it seemed like half the town was there. The crowd stretched into the street in both directions. For Ransom, it was exciting just to be there, and even more so to be in the scene, himself. And what happiness he felt when he looked out and there was Jenny, holding the hand of her mother.

The pastor opened the event in prayer, and then explained that over the previous nights they had considered the Old Testament prophecies about the One who would come—the Messiah, Christ, the Prince of Peace who, if we stayed our minds on him, would give us that peace no matter what our situation might be.

"Tonight we conclude this year's presentation with

readings again from the New Living Translation, in the gospel of Luke."

> *At that time the Roman emperor, Augustus, decreed that a census should be taken throughout the Roman Empire. (This was the first census taken when Quirinius was governor of Syria.) All returned to their own ancestral towns to register for this census. And because Joseph was a descendant of King David, he had to go to Bethlehem in Judea, David's ancient home. He traveled there from the village of Nazareth in Galilee. He took with him Mary, to whom he was engaged, who was now expecting a child.*
>
> *And while they were there, the time came for her baby to be born. She gave birth to her firstborn son. She wrapped him snugly in strips of cloth and laid him in a manger, because there was no lodging available for them.*

That night there were shepherds staying in the fields nearby, guarding their flocks of sheep. Suddenly, an angel of the Lord appeared among them, and the radiance of the Lord's glory surrounded them. They were terrified, but the angel reassured them. "Don't be afraid!" he said. "I bring you good news that will bring great joy to all people. The Savior—yes, the Messiah, the Lord—has been born today in Bethlehem, the city of David! And you will recognize him by this sign: You will find a baby wrapped snugly in strips of cloth, lying in a manger."

Suddenly, the angel was joined by a vast host of others—the armies of heaven—praising God and saying,

> *"Glory to God in highest heaven,*
> *and peace on earth to those*
> *with whom God is pleased."*

When the angels had returned to heaven, the

shepherds said to each other, "Let's go to Bethlehem! Let's see this thing that has happened, which the Lord has told us about." They hurried to the village and found Mary and Joseph. And there was the baby, lying in the manger. After seeing him, the shepherds told everyone what had happened and what the angel had said to them about this child. All who heard the shepherds' story were astonished, but Mary kept all these things in her heart and thought about them often.

"What a great description!" the pastor exclaimed. Imagine being one of those shepherds, having the angel of the Lord appear in the middle of the night. I don't know about you, but that would have frightened me, as it did them. After all, it's one thing to believe in angels, and another to have one appear without warning. Then, to change amazing to overwhelming, imagine having that one angel be joined by a multitude of other angels, saying, 'Glory to God in the highest, and on earth peace, good will toward men.' Wow! Double wow! The sky must have been lit up like daylight, only it was angel light, because the angels in the Bible are powerful and beautiful and bright. Since we couldn't rent a real angel for our display, we'll just view the ones we have as symbols of the real thing.

"For the rest of the nativity story, we return to Matthew, chapter 2."

> *Jesus was born in Bethlehem in Judea, during the reign of King Herod. About that time some wise men from eastern lands arrived in Jerusalem, asking, "Where is the newborn king of the Jews? We saw his star as it rose, and we have come to worship him."*
>
> *King Herod was deeply disturbed when he heard this, as was everyone in Jerusalem. He called a meeting of the leading priests and teachers of religious law and asked, "Where is the Messiah supposed to be born?"*
>
> *"In Bethlehem in Judea," they said, "for this is what the prophet wrote:*
>
> *'And you, O Bethlehem in the land of Judah,*

*are not least among the
ruling cities of Judah,
for a ruler will come from you who will be
the shepherd for my people Israel.'"*

Then Herod called for a private meeting with the wise men, and he learned from them the time when the star first appeared. Then he told them, "Go to Bethlehem and search carefully for the child. And when you find him, come back and tell me so that I can go and worship him, too!"

After this interview the wise men went their way. And the star they had seen in the east guided them to Bethlehem. It went ahead of them and stopped over the place where the child was. When they saw the star, they were filled with joy! They entered the house and saw the child with his mother, Mary, and they bowed down and worshiped him. Then they opened their treasure chests and gave him gifts of gold, frankincense, and myrrh.

When it was time to leave, they returned to their own country by another route, for God had warned them in a dream not to return to Herod.

After the wise men were gone, an angel of the Lord appeared to Joseph in a dream. "Get up! Flee to Egypt with the child and his mother," the angel said. "Stay there until I tell you to return, because Herod is going to search for the child to kill him."

That night Joseph left for Egypt with the child and Mary, his mother, and they stayed there until Herod's death. This fulfilled what the Lord had spoken through the prophet: "I called my Son out of Egypt."

Herod was furious when he realized that the wise men had outwitted him. He sent soldiers to kill all the boys in and around Bethlehem who were two years old and under, based on the wise men's report of the star's first appearance. Herod's brutal action fulfilled what God had spoken through the prophet Jeremiah:

"A cry was heard in Ramah—
 weeping and great mourning.
Rachel weeps for her children,
 refusing to be comforted,
 for they are dead."

When Herod died, an angel of the Lord appeared in a dream to Joseph in Egypt. "Get up!" the angel said. "Take the child and his mother back to the land of Israel, because those who were trying to kill the child are dead."

So Joseph got up and returned to the land of Israel with Jesus and his mother. But when he learned that the new ruler of Judea was Herod's son Archelaus, he was afraid to go there. Then, after being warned in a dream, he left for the region of Galilee. So the family went and lived in a town called Nazareth. This fulfilled what the prophets had said: "He will be called a Nazarene."

The pastor paused for a moment to let the previous scenario described by Matthew sink in. "Obviously, not everyone was happy that Jesus, the Messiah, the Prince of Peace, the Savior, the King of the Jews . . . had come into the world. Some received him joyfully, as we've seen; some rejected him and even tried to kill him. And this pattern continued throughout his entire life. Here is the way the apostle John describes it."

In the beginning the Word already existed.
  The Word was with God,
  and the Word was God.
He existed in the beginning with God.
God created everything through him,
  and nothing was created
  except through him.
The Word gave life to everything
that was created,
  and his life brought light to everyone.

*The light shines in the darkness,
    and the darkness can never extinguish it.*

God sent a man, John the Baptist, to tell about the light so that everyone might believe because of his testimony. John himself was not the light; he was simply a witness to tell about the light. The one who is the true light, who gives light to everyone, was coming into the world.

He came into the very world he created, but the world didn't recognize him. He came to his own people, and even they rejected him. But to all who believed him and accepted him, he gave the right to become children of God.

Then the pastor said, "If you have never received Jesus as your personal Savior, and you want to do that now, come on up here to the front and we'll pray with you." A number of people moved forward, including children, teens, and adults. Some of them were weeping.

When all who wanted to get to the front had done so, the pastor said, "Pray this prayer in your heart: 'Lord Jesus, I recognize that I am a sinner and need to be saved. Thank you for paying the ransom that releases me from bondage to the law of sin and death. At this moment, I receive you into my life. Come in and help me become the person you created me to be.'"

But he didn't stop there. He continued, "If you know Jesus as your Savior, but you have been carrying a burden such as anger or bitterness or resentment, just give that burden to him now, along with the weariness that comes with carrying such a load, and he promised that he will give you rest. Pray this prayer with me, in your heart: 'Lord Jesus, I have allowed my emotions to control my attitudes for far too long. Right now I give them all to you: my anger, bitterness, resentment—everything that hinders my running the race of faith, asking you to control and guide me. Amen.'"

Now more people were weeping, including two who were already in the front row: Hank, the rancher, and Cassie, Jenny's mother.

"Mommy," Ransom whispered, "why are they crying. Isn't this supposed to be a happy time?"

"Some are weeping in sadness, and some are weeping for joy. Humans are like that."

Hank had made his way to Cassie, who was still holding Jenny's hand right in front of Ransom, who could hear every word.

"Cassie," Hank said quietly. "I want to apologize for the way I treated you when, well, when you became pregnant with Jenny, without first being married. I was wrong; we all were wrong for judging and even shunning you, when what you really needed was our support. Just being reminded of Mary's situation when she was with child and not yet married made me think of you. I wonder, could you forgive me?"

Cassie seemed dumbfounded that the wealthiest man in town and Chairman of the Elders of the church would humble himself in this way. "Of course," she stammered. "It was hard, very hard . . . but yes, I do forgive you."

Hank reached over and hugged both her and Jenny. Then he said, "Is there anything you need that I might be able to help with?"

Cassie looked down at Jenny, paused for a moment, and then replied, "Well, I haven't been able to give Jenny many gifts at Christmas, which has really bothered me. She's never complained, of course. But we've never even had a Christmas tree."

"We'll be sure she has anything she wants on Christmas morning, and you, also. Since my wife passed away, I've not had anyone to whom I wanted to give some of her things, and I didn't have the heart to sell them. We'll start with her jewelry, if that's okay with you. And . . . it's going to take a lot more for me to catch up to what I should have been doing all these years while you struggled to make it."

Cassie just stared at Hank, her mouth open, for at least ten seconds. And then she started to cry. Finally, when she could manage a few words, she said, "Are you sure? I mean, you don't have to. . . ."

Hank took her hands in his own, and, looking her straight in the eyes, replied, "Yes. . . . Yes, I do."

Then he paused and looked at Jenny. "And what would make this young lady happy?" Hank asked.

"What Jenny really wants, and the only thing she wants," Carrie replied for Jennie, "is for Ransom to come and live with us."

It only took Hank a split second to reply. "Of course, and not only so, I will provide all his feed and anything else he needs."

Now both Jenny and Ransom were dumbfounded. "Really?" Jenny asked, excitedly. To which Hank nodded his head. "And if you would let me be like your substitute Grandpa, I would like that very much."

Ransom looked up at his mother, who was grinning as much as a sheep can grin. "Mommy," he asked, "what does this mean?"

"Well, it seems that you are going to have a friend for life. Jenny loves you and you love her. You should have many years of fun together."

"But will I be able to come and see you?"

"I'm sure that Rancher Hank can work that out. So be happy, and don't forget to thank God, who made this happen. After all, he's still doing miracles today, just as he always has been doing them."

. . . or maybe not!

About the Author

Dr. David B. Biebel is a minister, author, editor, and publisher. He holds the Doctor of Ministry degree in Personal Wholeness (with distinction) from Gordon-Conwell Theological Seminary in South Hamilton, Massachusetts. Over a period of more than 20 years of his career, he edited two national magazines for Christian doctors; first, the *Physician* magazine for Focus on the Family, and then *Today's Christian Doctor* for the Christian Medical & Dental Associations.

Biebel has authored or co-authored twenty books, including the Gold Medallion winner *New Light on Depression* and one bestseller: *If God Is So Good, Why Do I Hurt So Bad*, which was recently revised and re-released, with questions for personal or group study. His first book, *Jonathan You Left Too Soon*, considered a classic in the field, was also recently revised and re-released by Healthy Life Press.

Dr. Biebel founded Healthy Life Press (www.healthylifepress.com) to help new authors get their works to market in a variety of formats.

Making God Visible

How to Make God Visible by being "there" for your brokenhearted friend. Chapters include questions for individual study or group discussion:

1. What to say when you don't know what to say
2. A loneliness that must be shared
3. An emptiness that must be filled
4. Healing the wounds on their own terms
5. Becoming your friend's soul-mate
6. Life goes on
7. What to do when you don't know what to do
8. Somebody to hold me
9. To tell the truth
10. Moving with the pain
11. Beauty for ashes
12. Seven habits of highly effective comforters

If God is So Good, Why Do I Hurt So Bad?
(25th Anniversary Edition)

This **25th Anniversary Edition** of a best-selling classic is the book's first major revision since its initial release in 1989. This new version features additional original material related to the conundrum of suffering and faith (with principles learned along the way), and chapter ending questions for personal or group use.

One of the most profound, empathetic and beautiful books ever written on the subject of suffering and loss.
~ Sheila Walsh

In this remarkable book, my friend Dave Biebel helps the reader understand exactly what's so good about God in the midst of suffering.
~ Joni Eareckson Tada

Healthy Life Press

Books, eBooks, DVDs

Denver, Colorado

A Small, Independent Christian Publisher with a big mission—to help people live healthier lives physically, emotionally, spiritually, and relationally.

For a downloadable PDF catalog of our resources, and access to free sample excerpts from our books, visit: *www.healthylifepress.com*

1-877-331-2766 | *info@healthylifepress.com*

www.ingramcontent.com/pod-product-compliance
Lightning Source LLC
Chambersburg PA
CBHW051248110526
44588CB00025B/2915